Roller Coasters

By Virginia Loh-Hagan

21st Century
Junior Library

Published in the United States of America by
Cherry Lake Publishing
Ann Arbor, Michigan
www.cherrylakepublishing.com

Content Adviser: Dr. Todd Kelley, Associate Professor of Engineering/Technology Teacher Education, Purdue Polytechnic Institute, West Lafayette, Indiana
Reading Adviser: Marla Conn MS, Ed., Literacy specialist, Read-Ability, Inc.

Photo Credits: © Paul Brennan/Shutterstock Images, cover; © John Williams RUS/Shutterstock Images, 4; © Marcio Jose Bastos Silva/Shutterstock Images, 6; © Paul Brennan/Shutterstock Images, 8; © ChameleonsEye/Shutterstock Images, 10; ©Kiev.Victor/Shutterstock Images, 12; © Cassiohabib/Shutterstock Images, 14; © Leonard Zhukovsky/Shutterstock Images, 16; © Ruslan Kerimov/Shutterstock Images, 18

Library of Congress Cataloging-in-Publication Data
Names: Loh-Hagan, Virginia, author.
Title: Roller coasters / by Virginia Loh-Hagan.
Description: Ann Arbor : Cherry Lake Publishing, [2017] | Series: Extraordinary Engineering | Includes bibliographical
    references and index. | Audience: Grades: K to Grade 3.
Identifiers: LCCN 2016032395| ISBN 9781634721646 (hardcover) | ISBN 9781634722308 (pdf) | ISBN 9781634722964
    (paperback) | ISBN 9781634723626 (ebook)
Subjects: LCSH: Roller coasters—History—Juvenile literature. | Roller coasters—Design and construction—Juvenile literature.
Classification: LCC GV1860.R64 L65 2017 | DDC 791.06—dc23
LC record available at https://lccn.loc.gov/2016032395

Cherry Lake Publishing would like to acknowledge the work of The Partnership for 21st Century Learning.
Please visit *www.p21.org* for more information.

Printed in the United States of America
Corporate Graphics

CONTENTS

Roller coasters were inspired by giant ice slides in Russia.

What Are Roller Coasters?

What goes up must come down. Roller coasters are thrill rides. They're at **amusement parks**. People ride in wheeled cars. The cars ride on tracks. Chains carry cars up a steep slope. Cars reach the top. They roll down. They follow the track. They drop, rise, turn, loop, and stop.

Many people think roller coasters are exciting.

There are two types of roller coasters. Wooden roller coasters move up and down. They sway. Steel roller coasters have twists. They go high. They go fast.

Engineers must think about **forces** that affect human riders. Forces change. People need to feel the changes so that their muscles respond. If not, they could get hurt.

Look!

Visit your closest amusement park. Look at a roller coaster. Is it made of steel or wood? How long is it? How high is it? How many loops does it have?

Stored energy is potential energy. It changes to kinetic energy.

How Do Roller Coasters Handle Energy?

Roller coasters don't have **engines**. They use potential **energy** from **gravity**. Cars are lifted to the top of the first hill. They collect energy this way. They store this energy. They have the most energy at the top. For big rides, engineers make bigger hills at the start of the ride. The first hills are the most important. This increases potential energy. Cars use their stored energy throughout the ride.

Gravity gives a downward force.

Cars go downhill. They go fast. They fall. Gravity pulls the cars down. Falling builds up energy. Stored energy changes to kinetic energy. Gravity is the force behind this energy. Cars zip around the tracks. Gravity keeps cars on the tracks. It keeps the ride going.

Cars at Canada's Wonderland can make it through loops because they have enough speed at the top of the loop.

How Do Roller Coasters Stay on Track?

Tracks control energy. They control how cars fall. Downhill tracks let gravity pull down the front of cars. This speeds up cars. Uphill tracks let gravity pull down the back of cars. This slows cars down.

Engineers design hills and loops. They make sure cars have enough speed. Too much speed causes cars to fly off tracks.

Roller coasters at Six Flags Discovery Kingdom use gravity and inertia to send cars along winding tracks.

People feel gravity. They're pushed into and out of seats. Engineers want people to feel these forces. They create loops. Loops build moving energy.

Human bodies resist changes in direction. Bodies want to go straight. They try to do so. But roller coasters change directions. **Inertia** keeps roller coasters moving when tracks are flat or uphill.

Think!

Think about the importance of safety. Why do roller coasters need to be safe? How do engineers make sure they're safe?

On the Thunderbolt at Coney Island, a 90-degree drop is followed by a loop, rolls, dives, and hills.

How Do Roller Coasters Stop?

Roller coaster rides don't last forever. They lose energy to other forces during the ride. Not all energy changes into moving energy. Some changes into **friction** or **drag**.

Engineers think about friction. They don't want rides to stop. After the first hill, they make other hills smaller. This is so cars can make it over the tops. They also design special wheels to reduce friction.

Roller coaster cars use a combination of wheels to move safely and smoothly.

Cars' wheels rub along tracks. This reduces friction. Friction resists motion. Wheels allow cars to go faster. This creates heat. Friction causes the heat. Brakes are built into tracks. They're used when cars reach the **landing pad** at the end of the ride. Brakes increase friction. This stops cars. Cars also resist air. This drag slows cars down.

Ask Questions!

Ask friends or family if they've ridden a roller coaster. How did they feel before the ride? How did they feel after the ride? Would they do it again?

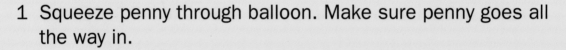

Try This!

Materials

clear balloon, penny

Procedures

1 Squeeze penny through balloon. Make sure penny goes all the way in.

2 Blow up balloon.

3 Tie off balloon.

4 Grip balloon at tied end. Hold bottom in your hand. Place fingers and thumb down sides.

5 Swirl in circular motion.

6 Watch penny. It may bounce at first. Then, it'll roll.

7 Wait for penny to spin. Use other hand to steady balloon. Penny should spin a bit more.